100 Visions and Dreams

OLAREWAJU OLADIPO

FOREWORD

100 Visions and Dreams is the fourth in a series of literary work of inspiration. At every stage of life, men and women are gifted with dreams and visions, many of which are fulfilled, many more of which go unrealized.

This companion book is a compilation of the writer's reflection on the uniqueness of visions and dreams, and the dynamics that dictate their outcomes. With the quotes on every page delivered in bit size, every sentence forces the reader to offer a personal interpretation of the message.

ACKNOWLEDGEMENT

This book is dedicated to all those who continue to support our work at 3SqMeals.

The person with a vision begins the journey of a lifetime with a deep conviction that the course to the destination is a navigable terrain. The person with a vision pursues the mission of a lifetime with a deep understanding that the ideal of the future is an achievable conquest.

There is no better way to establish independence of mind than with your imagination. You are not totally free until you free your imagination.

The big picture may lack clarity from afar, but don't be deterred by its lack of definition. A masterpiece is never revealed in a single stroke.

What is not seen has the power to cloud what you feel. A vision is felt well before it's visualized. Trust your instinct; pursue the unseen.

Many around you would like to express their belief in you, but they are all waiting to see you believe in yourself. Self-doubt is no option.

The worst enemy to have is the one that plays to your fear that you are incapable of achieving your dream—it's called the enemy of purpose.

In your dream you will solve the puzzle of who you are to become; in your vision you will solve the puzzle of why you need to become the person that you saw in your dream. To become who you are to be is to embrace your dream; to become who you are to mankind is to embrace your vision.

Everyone aspires to be what they can be, but many lack the will and the means. To be what you can be, you need to see the obstacles as real.

The joy of living is lost once we are consumed with finding our purpose in life. Finding your purpose is never a discovery but a revelation.

Hope is expecting the impossible to manifest in your reality. Faith is expecting your reality to manifest as you desire. Power your reality.

The 'power of one' is not in the ability that one person has to do good but in the multiplier effect that one person's action has on many others.

Many dreams do not turn out exactly as they were dreamed but often manifest in unexpected dimensions. Your dream is your encrypted reality.

Unless you make your world large enough to contain others, your world will never enlarge beyond your horizon. Make the world bigger for all.

Not everyone that has the ability to make an impact has the courage it takes to do so. Your thought is immaterial when your courage is zero.

A dream rarely comes to life until it is shared with others. To share your dream is to make it a dream for those who will keep hope alive. A vision rarely comes to life until it is shared with others. To share your vision is to make it a vision for those who will keep faith alive.

To achieve the uncommon, you need to respectfully acknowledge the obvious, actively engage the established, and vigorously pursue the unknown.

A misstep still counts as a step towards your journey on a personal adventure. Do not let a misstep put a stop to the pursuit of your dream.

The loss of a dream may be one's own doing or that of another person, but the loss of a vision is never the work of a third party. A vision may be sold or traded for a lesser ideal, but a dream can be lost or stolen. Your vision of the future is your responsibility to protect.

It is possible for more than one person to have the same dream, but it is impossible for two people to have the same dream at the same time.

You can either create an opportunity or wait for an opportunity. Waiting for an opportunity demands patience; creating one teaches patience.

To attain your fullest potential, you have to let your imagination set the rule and let your creativity be the judge of what is not possible.

May you find the courage to alter your ways and a vision to see clearly. May your new ways yield an outcome far better than your past years.

There are many years in a lifetime that many take a lifetime to mean forever. Whatever is finite has a span; whatever is limited has a worth.

No one individual who desire success sets out to fail, but many court failure by their unwillingness to do what it takes to become successful.

In your dream, your conscience
will be challenged; in your vision,
your belief will be examined. To
sacrifice one's conscience in the
fulfillment of a dream is to corrupt
one's dream; to forgo the ideals of
one's belief in the fulfillment of a
vision is to bastardize one's vision.

Many people desire to be defined by their victories, but the lasting victories in life are the outcome of a loss that redefines your purpose.

You don't need to think of yourself all day to discover who you are, but you need to think of the world all day to discover why you are here.

Dreams have no borders; visions have no territories. The territory of a vision is international, one that is accessible to the bearer irrespective of creed, age, or race. The boundary of a dream is endless, one that is accessible to the bearer irrespective of creed, age, or race.

If you are not taking steps every day to escape from the undesirable aspects of your reality, you will remain a prisoner of your circumstance.

You need not be rich to dream, but you need a dream to discover the richness of life. The richness of life is not defined by personal riches.

A dream is only as real as the people that bear witness to your dream. A vision is only as real as the people whose lives are changed through your vision. Many dreams remain unfulfilled, drowned in the sea of cowardice; many visions go unrealized, buried in the bed of self-doubt.

Passion may be a reason why you pursued a cause, but you need more than passion to finish the course. Without resilience, passion becomes undone.

The pursuit of a dream is no passive act—you not only have to explore the intricacy of your dream, but you become an embodiment of your vision.

Many leave our earth with unborn dreams; many depart our planet with untold visions. Dreams are born so that in their manifestation more dreams are born; visions are told so that in their revelation more visions are told. You owe it to this planet to birth dreams and see visions.

Know you are human first wherever you live. Consider yourself a global citizen and aspire to have an impact on a world beyond your locality.

There is no perfect time for the pursuit of the things that truly matter in life. Do not confuse the convenience of time with its perfection.

Every dream leaves the
bearer of a dream with one thing:
self-awareness; every vision leaves
the bearer of a vision with one
thing: meaning. Every dream takes
one thing from the bearer of a
dream: innocence; every vision
takes one thing from the bearer of
a vision: obscurity.

To master life, you have to master time. While some waste time in the pursuit of life frivolities, others pursue life for its timeless value.

Many exercise their freedom of imagination but fail to empower their imagination. Imagination without work only leads to a confused reality.

Dreams are never forgotten but may be suppressed; visions are never forsaken but may be subdued. A dream is a flame, every zone with a power of its own, strong enough to keep hope alive; a vision is a rainbow, every band with a color of its own, bright enough to light our paths.

Every human has a moment to contend with misery. What you do with your misery depends on you—you can either live up to it or give in to it.

No one has a right to judge another on the size of a dream, for the size of a dream is less of a barrier to success than the size of a heart.

Some dream may seem common until it becomes yours; some vision may seem ordinary until it becomes yours. The motivation to achieve the uncommon is what makes every dream unique to its bearer; the will to pursue the extraordinary is what makes every vision special to its bearer.

Every new day is a chance to see how wrong your prediction was about yesterday and recognize that you are no expert at predicting tomorrow.

The narrative of failure is best told when the success you so desire is no longer a distant dream but has become your much coveted reality.

Every dream is only as promising as its weakest link, every vision is only as hopeful as its weakest link. The weakest link in the fulfillment of your dream and in turning your vision into a reality lies in you, your attitude, your belief, and your fears. It is called the human factor.

The power to change your future is real but unrealized by many. The price to change your future is dear but not as dear as if you do nothing.

Never let the thought of getting it wrong scare you from making a bold move. The most well-thought out of human action is flawed by default.

The perfect dream is often shrouded in imperfection until you choose to take a first step to uncover its mystery. The perfect vision is often wrapped in opacity until you decide to make a bold move to see beyond its camouflage. Imperfection is the substance of all things perfect.

Your dream is often a reflection of your horizon. To dream big, you may have to alter your horizon. Your dream is only as big as you make it.

No matter how motivated you are to fully shape your destiny, there is an element of chance in the kind of ball that life throws in your path.

The price of a dream is never measured in a currency that is familiar to man, but in the elements of the soul that powered a dream into existence. The worth of a vision is never weighed with a scale that is familiar to man but by the impact that is yet to be experienced by many.

If every endeavor you pursue in life are ones with zero risk of failure, your success may be ensured, but you may never reach your potential.

You own your dream; don't let it own you. You work your dream; don't let it work you. The power to change your dream is what defines success.

The obstacle to a dream often lies deep in the heart of its bearer—an elixir of self-imposed limitations created by man and its environment. The hindrance to a vision often lies deep in the soul of its bearer—a plague of unsubstantiated fear rooted in self-doubt and cowardice.

If reaching the pinnacle of your life
means losing the thread of
humanity in you, you have
mistaken your real purpose for
existence on earth.

Not everyone is a dreamer, but we can all enable another person's dream. Many will fulfill their dreams while enabling other people's dreams.

There is no dream worthy of pursuit as the dream of personal freedom—a dream that is a birthright yet has to be aspired to be realized. There is no vision worthy of pursuit as the vision of personal freedom—a vision that is a privilege, yet has to be inspired to be realized.

You cannot teach ingenuity, but you can nurture creativity and instill perseverance. Not everyone is born a genius, but all are born to excel.

Do not confuse your dream with your fantasy. To fulfill a dream, you have to let go of fantasy. To live a fantasy, you have to forgo a dream.

Many spend so much energy seeking their purposes in life that they mistake their ambition for their calling. Allow your purpose to find you.

It takes an instant for a dream to take hold in the heart of a dreamer but many instants for a dreamer to hold on to the ideal of a dream. It takes a moment for a vision to play out in the eyes of a visionary but many moments for a visionary to play out the reality of a vision.

If your record of achievements is solely through your might, you may be cuddling mediocrity. Mighty feats often take a village to accomplish.

Many know what they want but
dare not place their winning bid.
Many know where they want to be
but dare not take a first step.
Dare to be.

Your vision may be clear, but the path is less clear until you fulfill your purpose. Your vision is yours to implement but for others to follow.

The substance of a dream is always timeless; the manifestation of a dream is always timely; the ideal pathway to a dream is always timed. The revelation of a vision is always timeless; the realization of a vision is always timely; the destined pathway to a vision is always timed.

The wonder of a worthy legacy is
that a journey of a lifetime is
shortened for many that follow,
not just to travel, but to take a leap
from.

Never expect a miracle where wisdom dictates that the outcome you desire depends on your sole effort. No one can dream their way to success.

A fool, overwhelmed with doubt over the ability to make a dream a reality, seeks a fortune teller in the quest for a foreknowledge of the future. A clown, inundated with fear over the will to make a vision a reality, seeks a soothsayer in pursuit of a foreknowledge of the future.

The sum of two halves of a dream shared between two persons working in disharmony is never equal to one. Nothing beats having a common dream.

To own your story, you ought to have lived it. To own your life, you ought to have dreamed it. To own your dream, you ought to have loved it.

Dreams may be broken, but a dreamer can always rebuild from the pieces; vision may be blighted, but a visionary can always sail past the obstacle. Dreams may be breached, but a dreamer can always mend the gap; vision may be guarded, but a visionary can always race past the fence.

When hope is your preferred line of credit, there is no limit to your cash withdrawal. The only collateral to access the bank of hope is you.

You possess the power to impart the life of another person in the time it takes to blink an eye. What you do with your power is your choice.

Every minute, a dream is born—an idea, a path, a thought, a victory, a clue, a journey, a friendship, a house, an expedition, a purpose, a job, an ambition, an aspiration, a goal, a mission, a vision, a feat, a decision, a resolution, a discovery—every minute a dream is born.

If you feel you have not fulfilled what you set out to achieve, you may have overlooked the opportunities that your disappointment presents.

In the pursuit of your heart's desire, be prepared for the unexpected. May your journey lead you to discover more than you have ever desired.

If you are smart enough to perceive your future, you should be brave enough to pursue it with zeal. Of what purpose is an unrealized future.

To dream is to counter the negative force that is inherent in the unpleasant experience of the past, to embrace the positive force that is hidden in the rare opportunity that the moment gives, and to deploy the neutral force that is latent in the real hope that the future offers.

If when you look into the mirror
of life what you see does not
match your dream, your reality is
distorted. Align your life
with your dream.

To have a vision is to have a hand in shaping your future. You may not eliminate the surprises in your future, but you can at least be ready.

Dreamers are less preoccupied with the thoughts of the number of obstacles that lie in the path to fulfill a dream but more preoccupied with the thoughts of the number of lives that their dreams will enable to overcome the obstacles that lie in the paths to fulfill their dreams.

You will never achieve the ultimate freedom that comes with meaningful work until you make the labor of work align with your innate purpose.

Having a vision is seeing past today's ordinariness—a world that is unfamiliar to many and considered by a multitude as impossible reality.

Hope is universal in its connotation but personal in its interpretation. To see hope manifest in a personal realm is to give hope to others.

A thousand dreamers, a thousand dreams. No matter how different our dreams are, we stand a better chance when we unite behind a common dream.

The echo of a dream often defies the human perception of sound. The image of a dream often defies the human perception of sight. The nearness of a dream often defies the human perception of touch. The sweetness of a dream often defies the human perception of taste. Dare to dream.

You have the potential to surprise yourself only if you try. You never know your true capability until you wholeheartedly pursue your desire.

When your journey is not just about you but a gateway to others yet to dream of their journeys, the burden of sacrifice is worth its weight.

To fulfill your dream, you need to turn desire into goal, convert wish into pursuit, change timetable into deadline, and make the future now.

If your dream is only a window to a multitude of dreams, to give up on your dream is to forgo the many dreams that are to follow your dream.

Passion has its limitations—alone it cannot deliver all the dreams that one desires. Passion driven by action is the ultimate dream-builder.

Unless you endeavor to see past time and prepare to explore the future, those whom the future belong to will inherit a future frozen in time.

To think in multiple dimensions, you have to turn your thoughts into images. When what you think is visualized, your thoughts become a dream.

A dream is a window into your heart, granting you access to that which is concealed and opening the well of creativity to those who thirst. A vision is a keyhole into your mind, granting you access to that which is concealed and stirring the flame of wisdom for those who yearn.

Inspiration is meaningless until you pursue that which others can only imagine. The surest way to stay inspired is to rule your imagination.

When your existence on earth is motivated by what you can endow it with more than what you can get out of it, you begin to live a life of legacy.

Do not be afraid to share your dream. It is in doing so that you will readily identify those who are for you and those who are against you.

Every true dream has life as long as it inhabits the soul of the dreamer; every true vision has life as long as it enlightens the spirit of the visionary. Behind every successful dreamer, there is a relentless soul; behind every successful visionary, there is a formidable spirit.

Whatever your pursuit is, do not stop in your track. The outcome is not always predictable, but you build a foundation for future greatness.

ABOUT THE AUTHOR

Olarewaju Oladipo is an author (fiction and non-fiction) whose writing career began while practicing as an orthopedic surgeon. Following the release of his earlier books "The White Coat" (2006) and "House Calls" (2007), he dedicated the next few years to crafting motivational quotes written using the Twitter handle @3SqMeals as Dr. O' and publishing multiple books under the '3SqMeals Tweets – Not Your Typical Meal' series.

His works of fiction include the "North Main Street" mystery series and the "Once A Doc" medical fiction series, with the release of Barber's Haven (2015), 'A Patient called Emma' (2015) and 'Ghost Bus (2016).

'The Sculpture Garden' series is based on actual sculptures and part of an ongoing effort to support the work of local artists in Nigeria, fund the establishment of sustainable sculpture gardens, and sponsor worldwide collaborations with art institutions.

Two Blind Men (2017) was the first of a collection of short stories of the 'Sculpture Garden' series. Tortoise of Many Colors (2017), The Tree of Wonder (2017), and Esther (2018) are other books in the series.

100 Prayers and Whispers (2018) is the first book in a series devoted to daily reflections of the author as shared using a dedicated Twitter handle - @3SqMeals.

All books are available in paperbacks and eBook formats on Amazon, Kobo, Smashwords, and on author's website (www.olarewajuoladipo.com).